D1643566

THE LITTLE BROWN BREAD BOOK

Recipes and ideas for a wide range of delicious breads with distinct character and real flavour.

THE LITTLE BROWN BREAD BOOK

by

David Eno

Illustrated by Clive Birch

THORSONS PUBLISHERS LIMITED
Wellingborough, Northamptonshire

This enlarged, revised and reset edition first published
1983
Second Impression 1984

© THORSONS PUBLISHERS LTD 1983

British Library Cataloguing in Publication Data

Eno, David
    The little brown bread book.
    1. Bread
    I. Title
    641.8'15   TX769

    ISBN 0-7225-0850-6

Printed and bound in Great Britain

CONTENTS

INTRODUCTION

In the first part of this book are recipes hints and information which should enable you to make consistently good bread. The second part contains ideas and variations to try once you have mastered the basic process, plus a selection of recipes for cakes and biscuits all using wholemeal flour and natural ingredients.

All the recipes specify 100% wholemeal flour although they could be used with ordinary white flour with equal success. However if you are going to the trouble of making your own bread and cakes there is little point in trying to emulate the sort you can buy at any baker's. Far better to use 100% wholemeal flour and make your baking full of flavour, and texture and with real character.

Wholemeal bread has been the staple diet of our land for centuries. For many the replacement of good hearty wholemeal bread with white tasteless, textureless sponge has been so gradual as to go unnoticed. The big commercial concerns have progressively forced the small bakeries out of business. By using factory production methods they can make and sell bread more cheaply. But, in order to make the whole process super efficient and super profitable everything has to be controllable and the flour is therefore refined and treated to remove all the variable elements. This ensures that one superloaf is identical to the next and that it remains moist and spongy down to the last slice. However this also removes many of the nutrients and much of the vitality of the flour.

Wholemeal flour milled from wholewheat grain contains not only the starchy white endosperm found in white flour, but also the germ and the husk. The germ gives wholemeal flour more protein, and fat, including essential fatty acids, more iron, thiamine, and riboflavin. The husk once thought to be unimportant because it is indigestible is a valuable source of roughage which is now recognized as being an important part of the diet, but which is, never the less, often lacking in the modern diet.

HOW BREAD WORKS

The basic ingredients are flour, water and salt, and unleavened bread is made just from these. This is too heavy for most people's taste and a lighter more spongy texture is favoured. This is achieved by adding yeast and a small amount of sugar upon which the yeast will feed, producing at the same time bubbles of carbon dioxide which blow up the dough and cause it to rise. The ability of the dough to trap this gas depends upon the gluten content of the flour. Gluten is a protein which forms elastic fibres in the dough and the more of it there is the more the dough rises. The soluble proteins and enzymes present in wholemeal flour have an unfavourable effect upon the gluten and therefore you can never obtain quite the same 'rise' as with white dough. Wholemeal bread is therefore more solid than white and you need to accustom yourself to cutting thinner slices or eating less.

White flour is favoured by the commercial baker because he can incorporate more water and more gas into the bread and make more loaves with less flour.

Wheat flour contains most gluten and is the flour most commonly used for breadmaking. The gluten content of different wheats varies. Canadian wheat is renowned for its hardness or high gluten content and is now widely used in this country for breadmaking. British wheats are softer (less gluten) and are not favoured by commercial bakers. The idea has grown up that they are unsuitable for bread-making. That this is not true is borne out by the fact that they have been in use for centuries and it is only in recent times that foreign wheat has been imported to any great extent. I mention this becuase if you are enterprizing enough to grind your own grain bought from a farm, or even to grow your own, the bread will not rise as much as with bought flours. It will however taste much better. (For information on how to grow grain see the various books on self-sufficiency by John and Sally Seymour.) When buying grain to grind make sure it is not intended for planting in which case it may have been treated with a poisonous dressing to prevent decay.

If you are buying flour then the ideal sort to get is compost-grown stoneground. This means that it is milled from grain which has been grown without the use of artificial fertilizers, insecticides, or any other chemicals. Stoneground flours are milled the traditional way with mill stones as opposed to high speed milling with steel plates. The temperatures involved in stone grinding are lower and this helps retain more of the nutritional qualities of the grain. Such flours are available under various brand names in health and wholefood shops and better supermarkets. Alternatively you can sometimes find a mill or bulk wholefood supplier locally which will supply 28 or 56 (12 or 25 kilo) sacks. Look in the 'Yellow Pages' for the addresses of these. Make sure about what exactly you are buying; preferably ask for or buy a sample first.

UTENSILS

Breadmaking requires the minimum of utensils. The basic necessity is a large bowl which can be bought quite cheaply from ironmongers and china shops. This should be at least ten inches (25cm) in diameter.

Plastic food mixing bowls are light, unbreakable and retain the warmth of the dough.

More pleasing but also more expensive pottery bowls can be bought from specialist kitchen shops. Measuring jugs, spoons and scales are handy but not essential. A most useful tool is a flexible rubber or plastic spatula with which the last remnants of the dough can be scraped from the bowl. Although flower pots, cake tins and a variety of other containers can be used for baking, or indeed, just a plain baking sheet for cottage type loaves, I find proper bread tins preferable as they produce a loaf which is convenient to slice.

Do not wash bread tins. If you oil them well with vegetable oil each time they are used they gradually develop a dark coating which is better than any non-stick finish. The same goes for baking sheets.

BASIC BREAD RECIPES

THE MASTER BREAD RECIPE

This method is known as the sponge method and is one which I favour because it is reliable and produces consistently good bread with most flours. It also requires minimal kneading and therefore takes less of your time. Part of its success is due to the yeast having almost ideal conditions for growth. During the initial sponge stage it is well supplied with air which is beaten in and it is not inhibited by the salt as in other recipes where this is added at the beginning. This method is also better for the formation of the gluten which aids the rising process and so is ideal for use with the softer British flours which may prove difficult to make into good bread using other methods.

Ingredients for 3 medium loaves

> 1½ pints (¾ litre) warm water
> 3 lbs (1½ kilos) approx. wholemeal flour
> ½ oz (15g) dried yeast or 1 oz (25g) live yeast
> 2 level tablespoonsful raw cane sugar or other sweetener
> 1 level tablespoonful sea salt
> 2 tablespoonsful vegetable oil

For the quantities given you will need a bread bowl

of at least 10 in. (25cm) diameter.

Ten steps to making good bread

1. Warm the bread bowl with warm water. Put
   1½ pints (¾ litre) of water in the bowl. This
   should be at 110-115°F/43-46°C or hand
   hot. Do not use water above this
   temperature or the yeast will be killed.

2. Add the yeast and sugar and stir a little, but
   do not leave to stand.

3. Begin adding the flour straight away, stirring
   continuously and adding more flour until a
   thick creamy consistency is obtained. This
   is the sponge stage and should use about half
   of the flour. In this method the amount of
   water used initially determines the total
   amount of flour required as this is added
   until the correct consistency is achieved. As
   different flours vary in their capacity to
   absorb water it is impossible and
   unnecessary to give an exact quantity for the
   flour. Beat with a large spoon or whisk for
   a couple of minutes to incorporate as much
   air into the dough as possible, as this helps
   the action of the yeast.

4. Leave in a warm draught-free place to rise.
   In summer almost anywhere in the kitchen
   will be warm enough, but in winter a

warmer place is desirable. The top of an Aga or other solid fuel stove is ideal. The sponge should double in size during proving. This takes 20 to 30 minutes normally and should not be prolonged.

5. Sprinkle sea salt over the dough and pour in the oil. Now fold in more flour using a large spoon or spatula and working around the edge rather than cutting into the dough. Keep adding more flour until the dough becomes dry enough to handle.

6. Liberally dust your hands and the table with flour and turn out the dough. At this stage the dough may be in several small pieces mixed with dry flour. The object is to knead all this together into one solid lump. Keep adding more flour when necessary to prevent the dough sticking to your hands or the table. It should remain fairly moist and workable.

   The technique of kneading is easily learnt. Take the lump of dough and flatten it by pressing away from you with the heels of your hands. The dough now forms a rough circle on the table. Fold this in half back towards yourself to produce a semicircle (1 and 2) and turn it horizontally a quarter of a turn (3). Push down again and fold back repeating the same sequence of operations over and over again. Once learnt this can be done quite rapidly and with practice the separate actions merge into a continuous flowing process. Kneading is best done on a firm wooden or laminate surface. As soon as sufficient flour is incorporated into the dough stop kneading as too much will harm the gluten.

7. Return the dough to the bowl and leave in a warm place until it has doubled its size, which should take from 20 to 40 minutes. A simple way of testing if the dough is ready is to make a slight depression with the knuckles in the dough. If the depression remains then the dough is ready.

8. Compress the dough with a few kneading actions and cut into three portions. Press together the cut edges of each and work in so as to leave only one seam along the bottom of each loaf. Oil the tins or baking sheet well. If using tins the dough at this stage should half fill them.

9. Leave the bread in a warm place to rise again and when risen gently transfer to the centre of a freshly lit oven set at 425°F/220°C (Gas Mark 7). Do not open the oven while the

bread is cooking, at least until 20 minutes have passed, or preferably not until cooking is almost finished.

10. Cook for three quarters of an hour. Remove from the oven and leave to cool for a few minutes before attempting to turn out of the tins. Make certain that the bread is cooked by tapping the bottom of the loaf which should produce a hollow sound.

    If the loaf is difficult to remove slide a knife around the edges. Once the tins have been used a few times there should be no trouble with sticking. It is a good idea to oil and bake new tins empty a few times. Cool the bread on top of the tins, or on a wire rack. If a thick crust is preferred on all sides the loaf can be returned to the oven for five minutes without the tin. Do not attempt to slice until barely warm. For best results do not leave any of the rising stages for too long. The minimum rising time always gives better results.

Summary of the instructions

1. Warm the bowl and put in 1½ pints (¾ litre) of hand hot water.

2. Stir in ½ oz (15g) dried yeast and 2

17

tablespoonsful of sugar.

3. Keep stirring and adding flour until a thick creamy consistency is achieved then beat.

4. Leave to rise for 20 to 40 minutes in a warm place.

5. Sprinkle 1 level tablespoonful of salt over the dough and pour over 2 tablespoonsful of oil. Fold in more flour until a hand-workable consistency is obtained.

6. With well-floured hands and table turn out dough and knead in more flour until a moist, workable, but non-sticky lump of dough is formed.

7. Return dough to bowl and leave for 20 to 40 minutes till double in size.

8. Divide the dough and form into loaves, folding under the cut edges and placing in well-oiled tins or on a baking sheet.

9. Leave to rise again for 20-40 minutes and then gently place in the middle of a moderately hot oven, 425°F/220°C (Gas Mark 7) for 45 minutes.

10. Cool on a wire tray.

Faults

If bread is crumbly in the centre it needs more cooking at a slightly higher temperature. This tends to happen with very large loaves.

If the bread is leathery try reducing the temperature a little.

If the bread is burnt on the top, but uncooked inside try reducing the temperature next time and put on a lower shelf in the oven.

With gas stoves avoid placing tins directly above the flame or part of the loaf may be burnt or overdone.

DECORATIVE TOPPINGS

To brown the bread brush the top of the loaf with milk. For a more glossy finish use an egg wash made from one egg beaten into a quarter of a cup of milk.

Various seeds can be stuck onto the top of the loaf using milk or egg wash. These add extra appeal and an interesting flavour. Try the following: poppy seed, sesame seed, cracked or whole wheat (soaked), sunflower seed, caraway seed, celery seed or linseed.

ROLLS

Follow the basic instructions but roll out the dough into a sausage shape and divide into a number of small lumps, bearing in mind that they will double in size. Cook for only 20 minutes at the top of the oven set at 425°F/220°C (Gas Mark 7). The advantage of rolls is that they are cooked more quickly and can be served almost straight from the oven if you are in a hurry.

PLAITED LOAF

When the dough is ready for the final proving divide one loaf portion into three equal-sized smaller lumps and roll into sausages about 18 in. (45 cm) long. Press these together at one end and carefully plait joining the other ends in the same way. Leave to rise and then brush over some egg wash and sprinkle liberally with poppy seeds. Put into the oven at the same temperature as the rest of the bread but remove after about 30 minutes.

FLOWERPOT LOAF

Bread can be baked in ordinary pottery flower pots and this gives it a delicious thick crust which looks most appetizing. It is best to buy a new flowerpot about 5 in. (12cm) in diameter. The shallow type of pot is best. Well oil and bake empty three times before using. Do not overfill or your loaf will end up in an awkward shape, unless of course you prefer a tall thin loaf!

LINSEED BREAD

Linseed adds a delicious oily, nutty flavour to bread. You can buy it very cheaply at a pet shop and it should be reasonably clean although it would be safest to give it a wash in a sieve under the cold tap. Dry by spreading over a clean tea towel. Add the seeds with the second half of the flour at stage five.

USING OTHER FLOURS

So far only wholewheat flour has been mentioned. There are of course a variety of other flours to choose from although it is usually best to incorporate a certain amount of wheat flour which ever one is used. This is because all other flours have less gluten than wheat and do not rise as well. Rye and barley do have a fair amount and can be used alone to make a heavy, moist bread. Maize and buckwheat flour have none and must be mixed with some wheat flour. If you use about half and half you combine the good rising properties of the wheat with the interesting variation in texture and taste of the other.

It is best to use the wheat flour to make the sponge and to add the other flour later. The following can also be tried: barley, soya, rice, maize, buckwheat.

WHOLEGRAIN BREAD

Whole grains are an interesting addition and produce what is sometimes sold as granary bread. Soak wheat, barley or rye grains for at least twelve hours. Use 1 cupful of dry grains to about 1 lb (½ kilo) flour.

ENRICHED BREADS

Eggs, milk, oils and fats can all be added to enrich bread. The water in the recipe can be all or partly replaced with scalded milk or dried milk powder can be added to the water.

An egg or two can be beaten in with the water and extra vegetable oil or peanut butter can also be added. These additions tend to make the bread more smooth and moist giving it a cake-like quality.

OTHER ADDITIONS

As you will begin to see the additions which can be made to the basic dough are almost unlimited and if you use your imagination you may be able to evolve something quite new. Here is a short list of additions to give you some more ideas:

Chopped nuts, sunflower seeds, dried fruit, sesame seeds, rolled oats, bran, cooked rice, cooked potato (mashed), grated apple or carrot, malt extract.

HERB BREAD (I)

Take some of the dough from the master recipe and for each 1 lb (½ kilo) loaf add up to 6 tablespoonsful of freshly chopped herbs. Use a single herb or a mixture. Try: basil, chives, fennel, marjoram, parsley, rosemary (in moderation), tarragon, or thyme. Also a clove or two of garlic can be crushed up and added to the dough.

HERB BREAD (II)

Pre-heat the oven to 350°F/180°C (Gas Mark 4). This is made with bread which is already cooked. It works well with long French-style loaves although it can be equally successful with crusty rolls or slices from a larger loaf. Melt 2 oz (50g) of butter in a saucepan and add a few finely chopped spring onions and a chopped sprig each of basil, marjoram and parsley. If using a French loaf then split down the middle and spoon in the mixture from end to end. Wrap in cooking foil and bake for 10 minutes. Cut into sections and serve straight away. Particularly good for soup and also for barbecues. If using rolls proceed as above. With thick slices of bread spread the herb/butter mixture and sandwich two slices together before baking.

PIZZA

Pizza is so easy and is everyone's favourite. It goes down well no matter if the weather is hot or cold. Although it is usually made with a special white dough I find that ordinary 100% bread dough makes a most acceptable pizza and is very little trouble to make if you save some dough when bread making. This keeps well on a saucer in the fridge for a day or so. This recipe is for Pizza Napolitana.

Ingredients for two good-sized pizzas:

> ¾ lb (350g) bread dough
> 3 medium onions, chopped
> 2 cloves garlic, chopped
> 2 tablespoonsful vegetable oil
> 1½ lb (¾ kilo) fresh, peeled tomatoes or
>   1 tin tomatoes
> Sea salt and freshly ground pepper
> 2 tablespoonsful oregano
> 4 oz (100g) olives
> 6 oz (150g) cheese, grated

1. Divide the dough into two and roll out on a well floured board turning often to make sure it doesn't stick.

2. Well oil a large baking sheet and transfer the dough leaving in a warm place to rise for about half an hour while you attend to the filling.

3. Take a frying pan and fry the well chopped onions and garlic in a little oil. Before the onion is thoroughly cooked add the tomatoes and cook for a while over a low heat to evapourate some of the juice.

4. Season with salt and black pepper. Spread the filling over the dough then sprinkle with oregano and black olives.

5. Cook at the top of a pre-heated oven at 425°F/220°C (Gas Mark 7) for 15 to 20 minutes. Sprinkle on the cheese and return to the oven for a further 5 minutes.

6. Serve straight from the oven either by itself for a snack, or for a celebration add a side dish of fresh salad and a bottle of red wine. Hooray for pizza!

CLIVE BIRCH

SPECIAL BREADS

QUICK SODA BREAD

This is useful in emergencies when the bread runs out. It takes little time to prepare and produces quite edible results in an hour.

> *½ teaspoonful sea salt*
> *2 teaspoonsful baking powder*
> *½ lb (¼ kilo) 81% wholemeal flour*
> *1 tablespoonful soft raw cane sugar*
> *½ lb (¼ kilo) 100% wholemeal flour*
> *¾ pint (400ml) milk*

1. Sift together the salt, baking powder and 81% flour.

2. Add the sugar and the wholemeal flour and mix well.

3. Add milk little by little and stir until a light dough is formed. Avoid adding so much milk that the dough becomes sticky and unmanageable.

4. Take a well oiled bread tin and press the dough into it.

5. Bake for 45 minutes at 375°F/190°C (Gas Mark 5), remove from the tin and allow to cool.

SCOFA BREAD

This is the traditional Irish Soda bread and, although made from wholemeal flour, has a quite different texture and quality from wholemeal bread. I like it particularly for breakfast toasted or untoasted, with marmalade or eggs.

½ lb (¼ kilo) plain 81% wholemeal flour
1 tablespoonful baking powder
1 teaspoonful bicarbonate of soda
Pinch of sea salt
1½ lb (¾ kilo) 100% wholemeal flour
1 tablespoonful Demerara sugar
1 oz (25g) butter
¾ pint (400ml) of milk

1. Pre-heat the oven to 400°F/200°C (Gas Mark 6).

2. Sift the 81% flour together with the baking powder, bicarbonate of soda and salt.

3. Mix in the 100% flour and the sugar.

4. Rub in the butter until a fine breadcrumb consistency is achieved.

5. Add the milk, which should first be warmed slightly, and knead to form a stiff but smooth dough.

6. Place on a well greased baking sheet and shape into a round loaf about 8 in. (20cm) across.

7. Using a knife, cut twice into the top of the loaf to form a cross then dust with flour.

8. Bake for 1 hour, when the bread should have risen and be turning golden-brown on top. When cool the loaf can be broken into quarters for easy storage.

WELSH FRUIT BREAD

½ pint (¼ litre) warm water
1½ teaspoonful dried yeast
1 teaspoonful soft raw cane sugar
4 oz (100g) 81% wholemeal flour
¾ lb (350g) 100% wholemeal flour
3 oz (75g) polyunsaturated margarine
3 oz (75g) Demerara sugar
1 teaspoonful sea salt
1 teaspoonful ground mixed spice
1½ lb (¾ kilo) mixed dried fruit
1 egg, beaten
Honey

1. Take a bread bowl and warm it with hot water.

2. Add the warm (blood heat) water and beat into it the yeast and cane sugar.

3. Add the 81% flour and beat again until a creamy mixture results.

4. Put aside for 20 minutes in a warm place until the yeast begins to froth.

5. Place the 100% wholemeal flour in a bowl and rub in the margarine.

6. Mix in the Demerara sugar, salt, spice and fruit.

7. Now add the beaten egg and the yeast mixture and mix the ingredients together with a spoon as much as possible.

8. Turn onto a floured table and knead the dough thoroughly for a few minutes.

9. Place in a covered bowl and leave to rise in a warm place until doubled in size.

10. Knock out any large bubbles with a fist then knead again.

11. Divide into two and place in two well greased 1 pound bread tins.

12. Pre-heat the oven to 350°F/180°C (Gas Mark 4).

13. Leave in a warm place again until the dough rises above the rims of the tins.

14. Bake for 50 to 60 minutes then glaze with honey and leave to cool on a wire rack.

BANANA BREAD

3 bananas, overripe
Juice of 1 lemon
4 oz (100g) soft raw cane sugar
4 oz (100g) polyunsaturated margarine
10 oz (300g) wholemeal flour
2 oz (50g) wheatgerm
½ teaspoonful sea salt
½ teaspoonful baking powder
½ teaspoonful bicarbonate of soda

1. Pre-heat the oven to 375°F/190°C (Gas Mark 5).

2. Mash the bananas with a fork until smooth and mix in the lemon juice.

3. Cream the sugar and margarine together then mix in the bananas.

4. Sift the dry ingredients together in a separate bowl.

5. Mix the bananas with the dry ingredients and form into a stiff dough.

6. Place in a well greased bread tin and bake for 45 minutes or until done. Test with a knife which should emerge clean when the loaf is done.

WHOLEMEAL MALT LOAF

½ teaspoonful sea salt
1 lb (½ kilo) wholemeal flour
½ oz (15g) polyunsaturated margarine
2 tablespoonsful molasses
4 oz (100g) malt extract
½ pint (¼ litre) warm water
4 oz (100g) sultanas
2 teaspoonsful baking powder

1. Pre-heat the oven to 350°F/180°C (Gas Mark 4).

2. Mix the salt with the flour then rub in the margarine until the mixture has a crumbly texture.

3. In a separate bowl mix the molasses, yeast extract and water, stirring until dissolved.

4. Mix together the liquid, flour and sultanas and stir well.

5. Leave for 1 hour in a warm place.

6. Sprinkle in the baking powder and stir again very thoroughly.

7. Place the dough in a greased bread tin and bake for 1½ hours.

BARM BRACK

This is a cross between a bread and a cake — not oversweet but moist, succulent and wholesome and very easy to make. Save the remains of a few pots of tea. Earl Gray is particularly good though any will do.

7 oz (200g) soft raw cane sugar
¾ lb (350g) mixed dried fruit
⅔ pint (350ml) cold tea
10 oz (300g) wholemeal flour
2 teaspoonsful baking powder
1 egg

1. Soak the sugar and dried fruit in the tea overnight. (Use a cloth or plate to cover.)

2. Sift the flour and baking powder together thoroughly.

3. Add the tea mixture to the flour.

4. Beat the egg in a separate bowl then add and mix well until a uniform mixture results.

5. Place in a well greased 2 pound (1 kilo) bread tin and bake for about 1¾ hours at 350°F/180°C (Gas Mark 4).

6. Allow to cool before slicing. Serve spread with butter.

USING UP STALE BREAD

You will probably be loath to throw away your own home made bread, and indeed it is much too good to waste, so here are a few suggestions for using it up.

Croûtons
Fry thick slices of the bread in vegetable oil and when crisp and brown cut into ½ in. (1 cm) cubes. Sprinkle over soup just before serving.

Breadcrumbs
Cut the bread into slices and dry very slowly in a low oven. When completely dry break into small pieces and grind in a liquidizer or fold in a cloth and beat with a rolling pin. Alternatively put the stale bread through a mincer and dry the crumbs on a baking sheet. As long as the breadcrumbs are absolutely dry they will keep for serveral weeks in an airtight container.

SUMMER PUDDING

This recipe uses up stale wholemeal bread and whatever soft fruit is available which can be black or red currants, raspberries, loganberries, blackberries or any mixture of these.

6 slices stale wholemeal bread
2 oz (50g) soft fruit
6 oz (150g) Demerara sugar
¼ pint (150ml) double cream to serve

1. Cut the bread, which should not be too stale, into medium thick slices and line a 2 pint (1 litre) bowl or basin with it, cutting to fit where necessary so that there are no gaps.

2. Wash the fruit in a colander under cold running water. Allow to drain and then place in a pan without any additional water and stew until the juice begins to flow. Add sugar as required.

3. Pour the fruit into the basin until it is full and then cut further pieces of bread to cover the top. Find a plate which just fits inside the dish and place a small weight on it. (The weight from a set of kitchen scales is ideal but wrap in a plastic bag to prevent the juice, which will overflow, from becoming contaminated.)

4. Leave in the fridge overnight or for several hours at least. When ready to eat it should have set fairly solidly.

5. To serve turn upside down onto a plate and decorate with fresh cream.

BREAD AND BUTTER PUDDING

This simple and homely pudding can be surprisingly delicious when made properly.

6 slices stale wholemeal bread
2 oz (50g) butter or margarine
½ lb (¼ kilo) raisins or sultanas
Grated peel of 1 lemon
2 eggs
¾ pint (400ml) milk
1 to 2 tablespoonsful raw cane sugar

1. Butter the bread on both sides and grease an ovenproof dish.

2. Arrange the bread in layers with the raisins and the grated lemon peel between.

3. Beat the egg, milk and sugar until the sugar is dissolved. Pour slowly over the bread and allow to stand for 1 hour.

4. Bake in a slow oven at 300°F/150°C (Gas Mark 2) for 1 hour.

Note: A good variation is to add sliced banana with the raisins.

CAKES, SCONES AND BISCUITS

FLAPJACKS

The quantities given for this recipe are fairly large and can of course be halved, but I find that flapjacks last no time at all unless strict rationing is imposed!

½ lb (¼ kilo) butter or margarine
6 oz (150g) Barbados or raw cane sugar
¼ teaspoonful sea salt
¾ lb (350g) rolled porridge oats

1. Melt the butter in a pan over a low heat and stir in the sugar.

2. Mix the salt with the oats in a mixing bowl and then stir in the contents of the pan and knead.

3. Press into a shallow baking tin and top with sesame seeds if liked.

4. Bake in an oven at 350°F/180° C (Gas Mark 4) for 15 to 20 minutes or until light brown on top.

5. Mark out the portions with a knife but do not turn out until completely cool.

OAT CRUNCH

6 tablespoonsful vegetable oil
3 tablespoonsful malt extract
2 oz (50g) Barbados sugar
½ lb (¼ kilo) rolled porridge oats
2 tablespoonsful sesame seeds, roasted
Pinch of sea salt

1. Pre-heat the oven to 350°F/180°C (Gas Mark 4).

2. Warm the oil, malt extract and sugar in a saucepan over a gentle heat. Remove from the heat and add the rest of the ingredients, mixing thoroughly.

3. Press into a shallow, square cake tin making a ½ in (1 cm) layer and smooth the top with a spoon.

4. Bake for 20 to 25 minutes and then remove from the oven. Mark out into fingers with a knife.

5. Allow to cool completely before removing.

PLAIN WHOLEMEAL BISCUITS

4 oz (100g) Demerara sugar
4 oz (100g) butter
1 egg
½ lb (¼ kilo) wholemeal flour

1. Pre-heat the oven to 375°F/190°C (Gas Mark 5).

2. Cream the sugar and butter. Beat the egg in a separate bowl and then mix with the sugar and butter.

3. Stir in the flour and mix to form a uniform dough. Roll out on a floured board and make into biscuits with a cutter.

4. Bake at the top of the oven for 10 minutes.

Variation: add 2 oz (50g) of chopped nuts to the above.

SESAME SQUARES

4 tablespoonsful set honey
4 oz (100g) sesame seeds
4 oz (100g) milk powder (freeze dried)
4 oz (100g) desiccated coconut
2 tablespoonsful peanut butter, crunchy

1. Melt the honey in a saucepan and then remove from the heat and stir in the other ingredients.

2. When thoroughly mixed pour into a shallow tray and refrigerate until set.

SCONES

1 teaspoonful sea salt
¾ lb (350g) wholemeal flour
2 oz (50g) polyunsaturated margarine
¼ pint (150ml) milk

1. Pre-heat the oven to 450°F/230°C (Gas Mark 8).

2. Mix the salt and flour together and rub in the margarine until thoroughly mixed.

3. Add the milk to form a stiff dough and knead for five minutes.

4. Roll out on a floured board and form into scones. Bake for 20 minutes.

5. Serve hot or cold.

CLIVE BIRCH

WHOLEMEAL FRUIT CAKE

4 oz (100g) 100% wholemeal flour
4 oz (100g) 81% wholemeal flour
¼ teaspoonful sea salt
1 teaspoonful baking powder
¼ teaspoonful cinnamon, ground
4 oz (100g) polyunsaturated margarine
   or butter
4 oz (100g) Barbados sugar
2 oz (50g) ground almonds
4 oz (100g) raisins
2 oz (50g) currants
1 egg
¼ pint (150ml) milk

1. Pre-heat the oven to 325°F/170°C (Gas Mark 3).

2. Mix the flours, the salt, baking powder and cinnamon.

3. Rub in the margarine or butter and then stir in the sugar, ground almonds and the dried fruit.

4. In a separate bowl beat the egg and milk together. Stir well into the main mixture and stir for several minutes until the ingredients are thoroughly combined.

5. Oil or grease a cake tin and spoon in the mixture.

6. Bake for 1 ½ hours and then test with a knife. Continue to bake until done.

MUESLI CAKE

This cake varies according to which muesli you use. I prefer the varieties with less sugar and plenty of nuts and dried fruit.

7 oz (200g) muesli
4 oz (100g) Barbados sugar
6 oz (150g) sultanas or raisins
2 tablespoonsful malt extract
½ pint (¼ litre) apple juice
2 eggs
2 cooking apples
6 oz (150g) wholemeal flour
3 tablespoonsful baking powder
A few whole almonds or walnuts for topping

1. Pre-heat the oven to 350°F/180°C (Gas Mark 4).

2. Take a mixing bowl and soak the muesli, sugar, sultanas and malt extract in the apple juice for 30 minutes.

3. Beat the eggs and add. Peel, core and grate the apples and stir into the mixture.

4. In a separate bowl mix the flour with the baking powder and then sift into the main mixture. Mix thoroughly.

48

5. Prepare a 7 to 8 in. (18 to 20cm) cake tin by oiling and lining with greaseproof paper. Spoon in the mixture and decorate with the nuts.

6. Bake for 1¾ to 2 hours. Test with a knife before removing from the oven.

7. Leave to cool for five minutes in the tin then turn onto a wire rack.

APPLE CAKE

2 oz (50g) soft polyunsaturated margarine
1 tablespoonful Barbados or dark sugar
¼ teaspoonful cinnamon
Pinch each of ground nutmeg and coriander
2 oz (50g) raisins
1 egg
6 oz (150g) wholemeal flour
¾ lb (350g) cooking apples

1. Pre-heat the oven to 350°F/180°C (Gas Mark 4).

2. Melt the margarine in a saucepan and then pour into a mixing bowl. Stir in the sugar, spice and raisins.

3. Beat the egg in a cup and add to the mixture.

4. Gradually add the flour mixing all the time and lastly the apples which should be peeled, cored and chopped into ¼ in. (6mm) pieces. The mixture should be thick and gooey!

5. Oil a cake tin and line with greaseproof paper. Bake for 1 hour.

6. Serve hot or cold with cream if liked.

HEALTH CAKE

4 oz (100g) wholemeal flour
4 oz (100g) walnuts, chopped
4 oz (100g) raisins
6 oz (150g) cooking apples, chopped
2 oz (50g) carrots, grated
2 tablespoonsful vegetable oil
1 tablespoonful brewer's yeast powder
2 tablespoonsful honey
½ tablespoonful mixed spice
Pinch sea salt

1. Pre-heat the oven to 350°F/180°C (Gas Mark 4).

2. Mix all the ingredients together and place in a large greased cake tin, making a layer about 1 in. (2cm) deep.

3. Cook for 20 minutes and then pour a little melted honey over the top. Cook for a further 20 minutes.

4. Allow to cool for five minutes before turning onto a wire rack.

MUFFINS

Hungry mouths to feed for tea and not enough bread or cakes? Muffins are quick and delicious! Use special muffin rings and a baking sheet for cooking, or any small tins about 3 in. across by 1 in. deep. For the best muffins give the batter the minimum of mixing. This quantity makes 12 muffins.

½ lb (¼ kilo) wholemeal flour
3 teaspoonsful baking powder
½ teaspoonful sea salt
3 tablespoonsful soft raw cane sugar
4 tablespoonsful polyunsaturated
   margarine
1 egg
½ pint (¼ litre) milk

1. Pre-heat the oven to 375°F/190°C (Gas Mark 5).

2. Sieve the flour, baking powder and salt together in a bowl, then mix in the sugar.

3. Using two knives cut the margarine into the flour until the mixture is granular.

4. Beat the egg and milk together in a separate bowl.

5. Make a depression in the centre of the dry

mixture and pour in the egg and milk.

6.   Mix just sufficiently to combine wet and dry ingredients into a batter.

7.   Spoon the mixture into greased muffin tins, filling to not more than ½ way.

8.   Bake for about 20 minutes when the muffins should come cleanly away from the tin and a knife inserted into the centre should also emerge clean.

9.   Serve hot with butter.

Variations:

FRUIT MUFFINS
Add 4 oz (100g) dried fruit at stage 2.

APPLE MUFFINS
Add 4 oz (100g) sultanas at stage 2 and beat in ½ cupful of cold stewed apple with the eggs at stage 4.

CHEESE MUFFINS
Reduce the margarine to 3 tablespoonsful and add ½ cupful of grated Cheddar cheese in its place.

BRAN MUFFINS
Substitute 1 cupful bran for 4 oz (100g) of the flour, 3 tablespoonsful of molasses for the sugar and add 2 oz (50g) of raisins at stage 2.

SPICY MUFFINS

To the dry ingredients add ½ teaspoonful ground cinnamon, ½ teaspoonful ground nutmeg, ½ teaspoonful ground mace and ¼ teaspoonful ground ginger.

JAM MUFFINS

Replace the sugar with 4 tablespoonsful of your favourite jam or marmalade.

BANANA AND WALNUT MUFFINS

Add 1 mashed, overipe banana and 2 oz (50g) of chopped walnuts to the basic recipe at stage 5.

INDEX